God's Little Instruction Book on Character

HB
HONOR
B O O K S

Tulsa, Oklahoma

God's Little Instruction Book on Character
ISBN 1-56292-076-6
Copyright © 1996 by Honor Books, Inc.
P. O. Box 55388
Tulsa, Oklahoma 74155

6th Printing

Manuscript prepared by W. B. Freeman Concepts, Inc., Tulsa, Oklahoma.

Introduction

Character has many different names and faces — all of them virtuous. We find all the highest and noblest aspects of character in the life of the Lord Jesus Christ.

One of the foremost reasons Jesus is our role-model for character is that His life on earth mirrored what He believed. We cannot espouse noble values, act in an ignoble way, and then count ourselves as having noble character.

We must choose to be the best we can be for God — to pursue the highest values, and then live our lives according to those values!

Our hope is that *God's Little Instruction Book on Character* will inspire you, "provoke you to good works," and help you develop moral excellence in your life.

What is Character?

In the home, it is kindness;
In business, it is honesty;
In society, it is courtesy;
In work, it is thoroughness;
In play, it is fairness.

Toward the fortunate, it is congratulation;
Toward the weak, it is help;
Toward the wicked, it is resistance;
Toward the strong, it is trust;
Toward the penitent, it is forgiveness;
And toward God, it is reverence and love.

For we are what he has made us, created in Christ Jesus for good works, which God prepared beforehand to be our way of life.
Ephesians 2:10
NRSV

Every human being is intended to have a character of his own: to be what no others are, and to do what no other can do.

Character is a byproduct. It is produced in the great manufacture of daily duty.

So I will sing praise to Thy name forever, that I may pay my vows day by day.
Psalm 61:8 NASB

Pride ends in destruction; humility ends in honor.
Proverbs 18:12
TLB

~

No amount of ability is of the slightest avail without honor.

8

W hen the late banker, J. P. Morgan, was asked what he considered the best bank collateral, he replied, "Character."

If you must choose, take a good name rather than great riches; for to be held in loving esteem is better than silver and gold.
Proverbs 22:1 TLB

The Lord searches every heart and understands every motive behind the thoughts.
1 Chronicles 28:9
NIV

~

Character is like a tree, and reputation is like its shadow. The shadow is what we think of it; the tree is the real thing.

It is more important to know where you are going than to see how fast you can get there.

It is not good to have zeal without knowledge, nor to be hasty and miss the way.
Proverbs 19:2 NIV

The Lord does not look at the things man looks at. Man looks at the outward appearance, but the Lord looks at the heart.
1 Samuel 16:7
NIV

~

Reputation is what men and women think of us; character is what God and the angels know of us.

Many a man's reputation would not know his character if they met on the street.

A good name is better than precious ointment.
Ecclesiastes 7:1
NKJV

~

Let your adornment be the inner self with the lasting beauty of a gentle and quiet spirit, which is very precious in God's sight.
1 Peter 3:4 NRSV

A golden character needs no gilding.

When we develop character we acquire lovely personalities, for personality is character shining through everything we do and everything we say.

Her ways are pleasant ways, and all her paths are peace.
Proverbs 3:17 NIV

Every prudent man acts out of knowledge, but a fool exposes his folly.
Proverbs 13:16
NIV

~

Character is made by what you stand for; reputation by what you fall for.

Dollars have never been known to produce character.

Better is a poor man who walks in his integrity than a rich man who is perverse in his speech and is a [self-confident] fool.
Proverbs 19:1
AMP

~

The lowly will be exalted and the exalted will be brought low.
Ezekiel 21:26 NIV

~

Many people have character who have nothing else.

We make a living by what we get, but we make a life by what we give.

By your standard of measure, it shall be measured to you.
Matthew 7:2
NASB

They need not account for the money entrusted to them, because they are acting faithfully.
2 Kings 22:7 NIV

～

A man's treatment of money is the most decisive test of his character — how he makes it and how he spends it.

If I take care of my character, my reputation will take care of itself.

The fruit of the righteous is a tree of life.
Proverbs 11:30
NIV

Charm is deceptive, and beauty is fleeting; but a woman who fears the Lord is to be praised.
Proverbs 31:30
NIV

~

'Tis beauty that doth oft make women proud; 'tis virtue that doth make them most admired; 'tis modesty that makes them seem divine.

Character is always lost when a high ideal is sacrificed on the altar of conformity and popularity.

Do not be conformed to this world, but be transformed by the renewing of your mind.
Romans 12:2
NKJV

Keep and guard your heart with all vigilance and above all that you guard, for out of it flow the springs of life.
Proverbs 4:23
AMP

Better to keep yourself clean and bright; you are the window through which you must see the world.

24

People are like stained glass windows. They sparkle and shine when the sun is out, but when darkness sets in, their true beauty is revealed only if there is light from within.

Let your light shine before men, that they may see your good deeds and praise your Father in heaven.
Matthew 5:16
NIV

How can a young man keep his way pure? By living according to your word.
Psalm 119:9 NIV

~

The most important thing for a young man is to establish a credit — a reputation, character.

It is better to be short of cash than to be short of character.

There is that maketh himself rich, yet hath nothing: there is that maketh himself poor, yet hath great riches.
Proverbs 13:7

When the way is rough, your patience has a chance to grow. So let it grow... then you will be ready for anything, strong in character, full and complete.
James 1:3-4 TLB

~

Character is a diamond that scratches every other stone.

Character must stand behind and back up everything — the sermon, the poem, the picture, the play. None of them is worth a star without it.

Whatever you do in word or deed, do all in the name of the Lord Jesus.
Colossians 3:17
NKJV

We do not need more national development, we need more spiritual development. We do not need more knowledge, we need more character. We do not need more of the things that are seen, we need more of the things that are unseen.

But seek ye first the kingdom of God, and his righteousness; and all these things shall be added unto you.
Matthew 6:33

Moral excellence comes about as a result of habit. We become just by doing just acts, temperate by doing temperate acts, brave by doing brave acts.

Learn to do good; seek justice, rescue the oppressed, defend the orphan, plead for the widow.
Isaiah 1:17 NRSV

31

Blessed is the man who perseveres under trial, because when he has stood the test, he will receive the crown of life that God has promised to those who love him.
James 1:12 NIV

Life is a grindstone. Whether it grinds you down or polishes you up depends on what you are made of.

You cannot dream yourself into character; you must hammer and forge yourself one.

We also glory in tribulations, knowing that tribulation produces perserverance; and perseverance, character; and character, hope.
Romans 5:3-4
NKJV

~

33

For whosoever will save his life shall lose it: and whosoever will lose his life for my sake shall find it.
Matthew 16:25

~

The cause, not the pain, makes the martyr.

Every man is the architect of his own character.

Whosoever heareth these sayings of mine, and doeth them, I will liken him unto a wise man, which built his house upon a rock.
Matthew 7:24

For precept must be upon precept, precept upon precept, line upon line, line upon line, here a little, there a little.
Isaiah 28:10 NKJV

Character isn't inherited. One builds it daily by the way one thinks and acts, thought by thought, action by action.

The essential factors in character building are religion, morality, and knowledge.

Jesus said to them, "You are truly my disciples if you live as I tell you to, and you will know the truth, and the truth will set you free."
John 8:31-32 TLB

Be strengthened with might by his Spirit in the inner man; that Christ may dwell in your hearts by faith... rooted and grounded in love.
Ephesians 3:16-17

Characters do not change...characters are only developed.

There is nothing so fatal to character as half-finished tasks.

Jesus replied, "No one who puts his hand to the plow and looks back is fit for service in the kingdom of God."
Luke 9:62 NIV

The man who had received the five talents went at once and put his money to work and gained five more.
Matthew 25:16
NIV
~

Whatever your lot in life, build something on it.

Character consists of what you do on the third and fourth tries.

Don't you know that this good man, though you trip him up seven times, will each time rise again?
Proverbs 24:16
TLB

41

The refining pot is for silver and the furnace for gold, but the Lord tests the hearts.
Proverbs 17:3
NKJV

~

No man knows his true character until he has run out of gas, purchased something on the installment plan and raised an adolescent.

Character is not in the mind. It is in the will.

...in all things willing to live honestly.
Hebrews 13:18

No discipline seems pleasant at the time, but painful. Later on, however, it produces a harvest of righteousness and peace for those who have been trained by it.

Hebrews 12:11
NIV

~

Another flaw in the human character is that everybody wants to build and nobody wants to do maintenance.

Every word and deed of a parent is a fiber woven into the character of a child that ultimately determines how that child fits into the fabric of society.

Be their ideal; let them follow the way you teach and live; be a pattern for them in your love, your faith, and your clean thoughts.
1 Timothy 4:12
TLB

~

Put things in order, listen to my appeal, agree with one another, live in peace; and the God of love and peace will be with you.
2 Corinthians 13:11 NRSV

~

Character is a perfectly educated will.

He who stops being better stops being good.

The righteous hold to their way, and they that have clean hands grow stronger and stronger.
Job 17:9 NRSV

Like a city breached, without walls, is one who lacks self-control.
Proverbs 25:28
NRSV

~

Many men have too much *will* power. It's *won't* power they lack.

I think character never changes; the Acorn becomes an Oak, which is very little like an Acorn to be sure, but never becomes an Ash.

Every good tree bears good fruit, but a bad tree bears bad fruit.
Matthew 7:17
NIV

Happy are those who do not follow the advice of the wicked...their delight is in the law of the Lord... they are like trees planted by streams of water... in all that they do, they prosper. Psalm 1:1-3 NRSV

~

Good, honest, hard-headed character is a function of the home. If the proper seed is sown there and properly nourished for a few years, it will not be easy for that plant to be uprooted.

What you dislike in another, take care to correct in yourself.

Take the log out of your own eye, and then you will see clearly to take the speck out of your neighbor's eye.
Matthew 7:5
NRSV

The genuineness of your faith — being more precious than gold that, though perishable, is tested by fire — may be found to result in praise and glory and honor when Jesus Christ is revealed.
1 Peter 1:7 NRSV

We often pray for purity, unselfishness, for the highest qualities of character, and forget that these things cannot be given, but must be earned.

Character is what you are in the dark.

Even in darkness light dawns for the upright, for the gracious and compassionate and righteous man.
Psalm 112:4 NIV

Serve Him with a blameless heart and a willing mind.
1 Chronicles 28:9
AMP

Our own heart, and not other men's opinions, forms our true honor.

54

Y ou are what you think about.

Lead every thought and purpose away captive into the obedience of Christ.
2 Corinthians
10:5 AMP

~

I will very gladly spend and be spent for you.
2 Corinthians 12:15

~

Character is the result of two things: Mental attitude and the way we spend our time.

Good habits are not made on birthdays nor Christian character at the new year. The workshop of character is everyday life. The uneventful and commonplace hour is where the battle is lost or won.

Do not turn to the right or to the left; remove your foot from evil.
Proverbs 4:27
NKJV

Encourage the young men to be self-controlled. In everything set them an example by doing what is good.
Titus 2:6-7 NIV

The discipline of desire is the background of character.

The inner braces of a man's heart must be equal to the outer pressure of life's circumstances.

Let us not lose heart and grow weary and faint in acting nobly and doing right, for in due time and at the appointed season we shall reap, if we do not loosen and relax our courage and faint.
Galatians 6:9
AMP

Just say a simple yes or no, so that you will not sin and be condemned for it.
James 5:12 TLB

~

Learn to say 'No'; it will be of more use to you than to be able to read Latin.

Merely going to church doesn't make you a Christian any more than going to a garage makes you an automobile.

I tell you the truth, no one can see the kingdom of God unless he is born again.
John 3:3 NIV

This above all: to thine own self be true, and it must follow, as the night the day, thou canst not then be false to any man.

A good man is guided by his honesty.
Proverbs 11:3 TLB

Character cannot be developed in ease and quiet. Only through experience of trial and suffering can the soul be strengthened, vision cleared, ambition inspired, and success achieved.

This short time of distress will result in God's richest blessing upon us forever and ever!
2 Corinthians 4:17 TLB

We are hard pressed on every side, but not crushed; perplexed, but not in despair; persecuted, but not abandoned; struck down, but not destroyed.
2 Corinthians 4:8-9 NIV

~

When duty calls, that is when character counts.

Character is built out of circumstances. From exactly the same materials one man builds palaces, while another builds hovels.

We are God's fellow-workers; you are God's field, God's building.
1 Corinthians 3:9
NAS

~

65

Those who are wise will shine like the brightness of the heavens, and those who lead many to righteousness, like the stars for ever and ever.
Daniel 12:3 NIV

~

It is an old saying, and one of fearful and fathomless import, that we are forming characters for eternity.

There is nothing truly great in any man — except character.

A little that a righteous man hath is better than the riches of many wicked.
Psalm 37:16

Whatever you do, do all to the glory of God.
1 Corinthians 10:31 NKJV

Our true selves are usually revealed in our seemingly trivial acts.

Men are not to be judged by their looks, habits, and appearances; but by the character of their lives and conversations, and by their works. It is better to be praised by one's own works than by the words of another.

Thus you will know them by their fruits.
Matthew 7:20
NRSV

And he [Judas] threw the pieces of silver into the sanctuary and departed; and he went away and hanged himself.
Matthew 27:5
NASB
~

If all the gold in the world were melted down into a solid cube it would be about the size of an eight-room house. If a man got possession of all that gold — billions of dollars worth, he could not buy a friend, character, peace of mind, clear conscience, or a sense of eternity.

If you think about what you ought to do for other people, your character will take care of itself.

Each of us should please his neighbor for his good, to build him up.
Romans 15:2 NIV

*They profess to
know God, but
they deny him by
their actions.
Titus 1:16 NRSV*

He does not believe who
does not live according
to his belief.

To enjoy the things we ought, and to hate the things we ought, has the greatest bearing on excellence of character.

A righteous man hateth lying: but a wicked man is. loathsome, and cometh to shame.
Proverbs 13:5

Dear children, let us not love with words or tongue but with actions and in truth.
1 John 3:18 NIV

People may doubt what you say, but they will always believe what you do.

Sports do not build character. They reveal it.

Do you not know that in a race all the runners run, but only one gets the prize? Run in such a way as to get the prize.
1 Corinthians 9:24 NIV

~

He who covers over an offense promotes love, but whoever repeats the matter separates close friends.
Proverbs 17:9 NIV

Never does a man portray his own character more vividly, than in his manner of portraying another.

A man of honor regrets a discreditable act even when it has worked.

A wise man's heart directs him toward the right, but the foolish man's heart directs him toward the left.
Ecclesiastes 10:2
NASB

77

So no weapon that is used against you will defeat you. You will show that those who speak against you are wrong.
Isaiah 54:17 NCV

~

When men speak ill of you, so live that nobody will believe them.

Do all the good you can,
By all the means you can,
In all the ways you can,
In all the places you can,
At all the times you can,
To all the people you can,
As long as ever you can.

Each one should use whatever gift he has received to serve others.
1 Peter 4:10 NIV

And those who are peacemakers will plant seeds of peace and reap a harvest of goodness.
James 3:18 TLB

Some people strengthen the society just by being the kind of people they are.

Persons with weight of character carry, like planets, their atmospheres along with them in their orbits.

He who walks righteously and speaks what is right...is the man...whose refuge will be the mountain fortress.
Isaiah 33:15-16
NIV

Thorns and snares are in the way of the obstinate and willful; he who guards himself will be far from them.
Proverbs 22:5
AMP

~

It is in trifles, and when he is off his guard, that a man best shows his character.

By nothing do men show their character more than by the things they laugh at.

Neither filthiness, nor foolish talking, nor coarse jesting, which are not fitting, but rather giving of thanks.
Ephesians 5:4
NKJV

He who oppresses the poor shows contempt for their Maker, but whoever is kind to the needy honors God.

Proverbs 14:31
NIV

~

The best index to a person's character is (a) how he treats people who can't do him any good, and (b) how he treats people who can't fight back.

Never does the human soul appear so strong and noble as when it forgoes revenge and dares to forgive an injury.

Never pay back evil for evil. Do things in such a way that everyone can see you are honest clear through.
Romans 12:17
TLB

Let each of you esteem and look upon and be concerned for not [merely] his own interests, but also each for the interests of others.
Philippians 2:4
AMP

~

Character: When you have the same ailments as the other person but refrain from mentioning it.

Character is not made in crisis — it is only exhibited.

When Joseph went into the house to do his work, and none of the men of the house was inside, ...she caught him by his garment, saying, "Lie with me." But he left his garment in her hand, and fled and ran outside.
Genesis 39:11-12
NKJV
~

Whatever you have said in the dark will be heard in the light, and what you have whispered behind closed doors will be proclaimed from the housetops.
Luke 12:3 NRSV

~

Live in such a way that you would not be ashamed to sell your parrot to the town gossip.

A lways do right. This will gratify most people, and astonish the rest.

Withhold not good from them to whom it is due, when it is in the power of thine hand to do it.
Proverbs 3:27

A friend loves at all times, and is born, as is a brother, for adversity.
Proverbs 17:17
AMP

~

Promises may get friends, but it is performance that must nurse and keep them.

The final test of a gentleman is his respect for those who can be of no possible service to him.

Love your enemies! Do good to them!...
And don't be concerned about the fact that they won't repay.
Luke 6:35 TLB

All the ways of a man are clean in his own eyes; but the Lord weigheth the spirits.
Proverbs 16:2

~

Every man has three characters: that which he exhibits, that which he has, and that which he thinks he has.

When a man thinks he is reading the character of another, he is often unconsciously betraying his own.

When you say they are wicked and should be punished, you are talking about yourselves, for you do these very same things.
Romans 2:1 TLB

~

Like a muddied spring or a polluted well is a righteous man who gives way to the wicked.
Proverbs 25:26
NIV

~

He that always gives way to others will end in having no principles of his own.

94

No man, for any considerable time, can wear one face to himself and another to the multitude without finally getting bewildered as to which may be the true.

Draw near to God and He will draw near to you. Cleanse your hands...and purify your hearts, you double-minded.
James 4:8 NAS

Let not mercy and truth forsake thee: bind them about thy neck; write them upon the table of thine heart: So shalt thou find favour and good understanding in the sight of God and man.
Proverbs 3:3-4

It is not the brains that matter most, but that which guides them — the character, the heart, generous qualities, progressive ideas.

Few people are made of such strong fiber that they will make a costly outlay when surface work will pass as well in the market.

Work hard and become a leader; be lazy and never succeed.
Proverbs 12:24
TLB

~

But ye, brethren, be not weary in well doing.
2 Thessalonians 3:13

Character is the total of thousands of small daily strivings to live up to the best that is in us.

A character standard is far more important than even a gold standard. In the last analysis, our national future depends upon our national character — that is, whether it is spiritually or materially minded.

If you will only obey the Lord your God, by diligently observing all his commandments... the Lord your God will set you high above all the nations of the earth.
Deuteronomy 28:1 NRSV

~

Blessed is the nation whose God is the Lord, whose people he has chosen as his own.
Psalm 33:12 TLB

America was built not by politicians running for something, but by statesmen standing for something.

The happiness of every country depends upon the character of its people, rather than the form of its government.

Where there is no vision, the people perish: but he that keepeth the law, happy is he. Proverbs 29:18

He who is faithful in what is least is faithful also in much; and he who is unjust in what is least is unjust also in much.
Luke 16:10 NKJV

~

Aware of the controlling power of ambition, corruption and emotion, it may be that in the search for wiser government we should look for the test of character first.

Leadership is a potent combination of strategy and character. But if you must be without one, be without the strategy.

Without wise leadership, a nation is in trouble; but with good counselors there is safety.
Proverbs 11:14
TLB

~

103

A righteous man who walks in his integrity — How blessed are his sons after him.
Proverbs 20:7 NAS

Decency — generosity — cooperation — assistance in trouble — devotion to duty; these are the things that are of greater value than surface appearances and customs.

Talents are best nurtured in solitude: character is best formed in the stormy billows of the world.

But he knows the way that I take; when he has tried me, I shall come forth as gold.
Job 23:10 NAS

He whose walk is blameless and who does what is righteous, who speaks the truth from his heart... He who does these things will never be shaken.
Psalm 15:2,5 NIV

Though goodness without knowledge is weak and feeble; yet knowledge without goodness is dangerous; both united form the noblest character and lay the surest foundation of usefulness to mankind.

The character that needs law to mend it, is hardly worth the tinkering.

We know that law is made not for the righteous but for lawbreakers and rebels.
1 Timothy 1:9
NIV

He who trusts in himself is a fool, but he who walks in wisdom is kept safe.
Proverbs 28:26
NIV

Not education, but character, is man's greatest need and man's greatest safeguard.

No man or woman can really be strong, gentle, pure, and good without the world being better for it.

You are the light of the world. A city on a hill cannot be hidden.
Matthew 5:14
NIV

...forgetting those things which are behind, and reaching forth unto those things which are before.
Philippians 3:13

Whatever disgrace we may have deserved, it is almost always in our power to reestablish our character.

Character is much easier kept than recovered.

But as for me, I will walk in my integrity.
Psalm 26:11 AMP

You should know that loving the world is the same as hating God. Anyone who wants to be a friend of the world becomes God's enemy.
James 4:4 NCV

People seem not to realize that their opinion of the world is also a confession of character.

It is easier to fight for principles than to live up to them.

Fight the good fight of faith. Take hold of the eternal life to which you were called when you made your good confession in the presence of many witnesses.
1 Timothy 6:12
NIV
~

If you are slack in the day of distress, your strength is limited.
Proverbs 24:10
NAS

~

A character that cannot defend itself is not worth vindicating.

When no wind blows, even the weathervane has character.

See, I have refined you, though not as silver; I have tested you in the furnace of affliction.
Isaiah 48:10 NIV

Shepherd the flock of God which is among you, serving as overseers, not by compulsion but willingly, not for dishonest gain but eagerly; nor as being lords over those entrusted to you, but being examples to the flock.

1 Peter 5:2-3
NKJV

Nearly all men can stand adversity, but if you want to test a man's character, give him power.

Character...is as potent a force in world conflict as it is in our own domestic affairs. It strikes the last blow in any battle.

When a man's ways are pleasing to the Lord, he makes even his enemies live at peace with him.
Proverbs 16:7 NIV

L ong-term survival depends alone on the character of man. We must remember that it was not the outer grandeur of the Roman but the inner simplicity of the Christian that lived on through the ages.

For the grace of God that brings salvation has appeared to all men, teaching us that, denying ungodliness and worldly lusts, we should live soberly, righteously, and godly in the present age.
Titus 2:11-12
NKJV

The great hope of society is individual character.

Righteousness exalts a nation.
Proverbs 14:34
NRSV

It's what each of us sows, and how, that gives to us character and prestige. Seeds of kindness, goodwill, and human understanding, planted in fertile soil, spring up into deathless friendships, big deeds of worth, and a memory that will not soon fade out. We are all sowers of seeds — and let us never forget it!

A man will always reap just the kind of crop he sows!
Galatians 6:7 TLB

The law of harvest is to reap more than you sow. Sow an act, and you reap a habit; sow a habit, and you reap a character; sow a character and you reap a destiny.

I press toward the mark for the prize of the high calling of God in Christ Jesus.
Philippians 3:14

Most important of all, continue to show deep love for each other, for love makes up for many of your faults.
1 Peter 4:8 TLB

It is easier to enrich ourselves with a thousand virtues than to correct ourselves of a single fault.

Character building
begins in our infancy
and continues until death.

*Even a child is
known by his
actions, by
whether his
conduct is pure
and right.*
Proverbs 20:11
NIV

I wish above all things that thou mayest prosper and be in health, even as thy soul prospereth.
3 John 2

~

It is the character of very few men to honor without envy a friend who has prospered.

Our character is but the stamp on our souls of the free choices of good and evil we have made through life.

Hate what is evil; cling to what is good.
Romans 12:9 NIV

O my son, be wise and stay in God's paths.
Proverbs 23:19
TLB

~

Fads come and go; wisdom and character go on forever.

When God measures a man, he puts the tape around the heart, not the head.

The only letter I need is you yourselves! They can see that you are a letter from Christ, written by us...not one carved on stone, but in human hearts.
2 Corinthians 3:2-3 TLB

And everyone who competes for the prize is temperate in all things.... to obtain a perishable crown, but we for an imperishable crown.
1 Corinthians 9:25 NKJV
~

Moderation is an ostentatious proof of our strength of character.

Good character is human nature in its best form...it is moral order embodied in the individual.

We have this treasure in clay jars, so that it may be made clear that this extraordinary power belongs to God and does not come from us.
2 Corinthians 4:7
NRSV

I have set the Lord always before me: because he is at my right hand, I shall not be moved.
Psalm 16:8

~

Character is long-standing habit.

An upright man casts the longest shadow.

The integrity of the upright will guide them, But the falseness of the treacherous will destroy them.
Proverbs 11:3
NASB

*Surely he will
never be shaken;
a righteous
man will be
remembered
forever.*
Psalm 112:6 NIV

Character needs no epitaph. You can bury a man, but character will beat the hearse back from the graveyard.

Manners carry the world for the moment; character for all times.

I would have you learn this great fact: that a life of doing right is the wisest life there is.
Proverbs 4:11 TLB

In a race, everyone runs but only one person gets first prize... To win the contest you must deny yourselves many things that would keep you from doing your best.
1 Corinthians 9:24-25 TLB

Character may be manifested in the great moments, but it is made in the small ones.

Personality has the power to open many doors, but character must keep them open.

*The righteous
shall never
be removed.
Proverbs 10:30*

No good thing does he withhold from those whose walk is blameless.
Psalm 84:11 NIV

Character is power; it makes friends, draws patronage and support, and opens a sure way to wealth, honor, and happiness.

It matters not what you are thought to be, but what you are.

The good man out of the good treasure of his heart brings forth what is good; and the evil man out of the evil treasure brings forth what is evil.
Luke 6:45 NASB

I beseech you therefore, brethren, by the mercies of God, that you present your bodies a living sacrifice, holy, acceptable to God.
Romans 12:1
NKJV

~

My business is not to remain myself, but to make the absolute best of what God made.

Rubber balls and character are alike in this way: they both rebound high.

He brought me up also out of a horrible pit... and set my feet upon a rock, and established my goings.
Psalm 40:2

One who walks in integrity will be safe, but whoever follows crooked ways will fall into the Pit.
Proverbs 28:18
TLB

A tree will not only lie as it falls but it will fall as it leans.

Only what we have wrought into our character during life can we take away with us.

Till I die I will not remove mine integrity from me. My righteousness I hold fast, and will not let it go: my heart shall not reproach me so long as I live.
Job 27:5-6

Though the tide of battle runs strongly against me, for so many are fighting me, yet he will rescue me.
Psalm 55:18 TLB

~

God will not look you over for medals, degrees or diplomas, but for scars.

142

A beautiful heart seems to transform the homeliest face.

He hath made every thing beautiful in his time.
Ecclesiastes 3:11

Yea, though I walk through the valley of the shadow of death, I will fear no evil: for thou art with me.
Psalm 23:4

The man of character finds an especial attractiveness in difficulty, since it is only by coming to grips with difficulty that he can realize his potentialities.

Character, not circumstances, make the man.

It was by faith that Moses, when he grew up, refused to be treated as the grandson of the king, but chose to share ill-treatment with God's people.
Hebrews 11:24-25
TLB

Those who spare the rod hate their children, but those who love them are diligent to discipline them.
Proverbs 13:24
NRSV
~

Many parents are finding out that a pat on the back helps develop character — if given often enough, early enough, and low enough.

If your absence doesn't make any difference, your presence won't either.

Ye are the salt of the earth: but if the salt have lost his savour, wherewith shall it be salted?
Matthew 5:13

Righteousness and justice are the foundation of Your throne; Mercy and truth go before Your face.
Psalm 89:14 NKJV

~

Truthfulness is a cornerstone in character, and if it be not firmly laid in youth, there will ever after be a weak spot in the foundation.

There is not a man or woman, however poor they may be, but have it in their power, by the grace of God, to leave behind them the grandest thing on earth: character.

A good man leaveth an inheritance to his children's children.
Proverbs 13:22

Store up for yourselves treasures in heaven...where thieves do not break in and steal.

Matthew 6:20

NIV

Remember that what you possess in the world will be found at the day of your death to belong to another, but what you are will be yours forever.

If there is righteousness in the heart there will be beauty in the character. If there be beauty in the character, there will be harmony in the home. If there is harmony in the home, there will be order in the nation. When there is order in the nation, there will be peace in the world.

Be at peace and live in harmony with one another.
Mark 9:50 AMP

The whole Bible was given to us by inspiration from God and is useful to teach us what is true...it straightens us out and helps us do what is right.
2 Timothy 3:16
TLB

The finest qualities of our characters do not come from trying but from that mysterious and yet most effective capacity to be inspired.

W̲e shall never wander from Christ while we make character the end and aim of all our intellectual discipline; and we shall never misconceive character while we hold fast to Christ, and keep him first in our motto and our hearts.

Being confident of this very thing, that He who has begun a good work in you will complete it until the day of Jesus Christ.
Philippians 1:6
NKJV

~

The righteous give and do not hold back.
Proverbs 21:26
NRSV

~

No person was ever honored for what he received. Honor has been the reward for what he gave.

References

Unless otherwise indicated, all Scripture quotations are taken from the *King James Version* of the Bible.

Scripture quotations marked NIV are taken from the *Holy Bible, New International Version* NIV. Copyright © 1973, 1978, 1984 by International Bible Society. Used by permission of Zondervan Publishing House. All rights reserved.

Scripture quotations marked NASB are taken from the *New American Standard Bible*. Copyright © The Lockman Foundation 1960, 1962, 1963, 1968, 1971, 1972, 1973, 1975, 1977. Used by permission.

Verses marked TLB are taken from the *The Living Bible,* copyright © 1971. Used by permission of Tyndale House Publishers, Inc., Wheaton, Illinois 60189. All rights reserved.

Acknowledgments

William Ellery Channing (6,119), Woodrow Wilson (7,71), Andrew Carnegie (8), Abraham Lincoln (10,116), Martin Vanbee (11), Thomas Paine (12,111), Elbert Hubbard (13,56,142), E. Maude Gardner (15), W.K. Kellogg (17), Don Herold (18), Winston Churchill (19), James Moffatt (20), D. L. Moody (21,53), Charles R. Swindoll (23), George Bernard Shaw (24), Elizabeth Kübler-Ross (25), John D. Rockefeller (26), Cyrus A. Bartol (28), J. G. Holland (29), Calvin Coolidge (30,154), Aristotle (31,73), James A. Froude (33), G. D. Boardman (35,121), Helen Gahagan Douglas (36), J. L. Pickard (37), Benjamin Disraeli (38), David Lloyd (39), James A. Michener (41), Mercelene Cox (42), Fulton J. Sheen (43), Kurt Vonnegut (44), David Wilkerson (45), Novalis (46), Cromwell (47), John A. Shedd (48), Hester Lynch Piozzi (49), George A. Dorsey (50), Thomas Sprat (51), Lyman Abbott (52), Samuel Taylor Coleridge (54), Maltbie D. Babcock (57), John Locke (58), Charles Haddon Spurgeon (60), William Shakespeare (62), Helen Keller (63), William Safire (64), George Henry Lewes (65), Burritt (66),L'Estrange (69), Charles F. Banning (70), Thomas Fuller (72), Heywood Hale Broun (75), Jean Paul Richter (76), H.L. Menken (77), Plato (78), John Wesley (79), John W. Gardner (80), Thomas

Hardy (81), Arthur Schopenhauer (82), Goethe (83,105), Abigail Van Buren (84), E. H. Chapin (85), Dr. Robert Freeman (87), Will Rogers (88), Mark Twain (89), Owen Feltham (90), William Lyon Phelps (91), Alphonse Karr (92), Joseph Farrell (93), Aesop (94), Nathaniel Hawthorne (95), Fyodor Dostoyevski (96), E.M. Bounds (97), A.G. Trudeau (98), Roger Babson (99), Vance Havner (100), Thomas Chandler Haliburton (101), Barbara Tuchman (102), H. Norman Schwarzkopf (103), Dwight D. Eisenhower (104), John Phillips (106), Douglas Jerrold (107), Herbert Spencer (108), Phillips Brooks (109,134), Titus Maccius Plautus (110), Ralph Waldo Emerson (112), Alfred Adler (113), F. W. Robertson (114), Stanislaw J. Lec (115), Philip D. Reed (117), Charles A. Lindbergh (118), George Matthew Adams (120), Jean de la Bruyere (122), Anna Eleanor Roosevelt (123), Aeschylus (124), John Cunningham Geikie (125), La Rochefoucauld (128), Samuel Smiles (129), Plutarch (130), J. Howe (136), Latin Proverb (137), Robert Browning (138), J. J. Gurney (140), Alexander Humboldt (141), Charles de Gaulle (144), Booker T. Washington (145), Jefferson Davis (148), Norman McLeod (149), Henry Van Dyke (150), Chinese Proverb (151), Harry Emerson Fosdick (152), Sylvester F. Scovel (153).

Additional Copies of this book and other titles in the
God's Little Instruction Book series are available at your local bookstore.

God's Little Instruction Book
God's Little Instruction Book II
God's Little Instruction Book for Mom
God's Little Instruction Book for Dad
God's Little Instruction Book for Graduates
God's Little Instruction Book for Students
God's Little Instruction Book for Kids
God's Little Instruction Book for Couples
God's Little Instruction Book for Women
God's Little Instruction Book for the Workplace
God's Little Instruction Book — Special Gift Edition
God's Little Instruction Book Daily Calendar

HB
HONOR
BOOKS

Tulsa, Oklahoma